THE POWER
OF CHILDHOOD

"It's time to break the self-destructive cycle of child-hood trauma in your life!"

LAWRENCE W. STANFIELD, Ph.D.

DEDICATION

This book is dedicated to the tens of thousands of adults, children and families that still experience the self-sabotaging effects of an unstable childhood. Although, most of us are not able to understand why our lives are anything but victorious and happy, it is my prayer that within these pages you will begin to discover healing and victory over present- day suffering from past childhood hurts and bondage.

CONTENTS

ACKNOWLEDGMENTS

The existence of this book owes a great deal of gratitude to the counselors, pastors, pioneers, and survivors of childhood abuse and trauma. The author acknowledges a great of indebtedness to the brave people who remained on the frontlines of in our world's secret warfare to *set the captives free*!

-1-
IS YOUR PAST YOUR PRESENT?

"The Lord is near to the brokenhearted and saves the crushed in spirit."
(Psalm 34:18)

> "Sometimes past hurts can be so overwhelming that you become preoccupied with them. Intrusive thoughts about those memories insert themselves into your mind, derailing you from effectively taking care of, or enjoying, your current life."
> (Leslie B. Phelps, Ph.D.)

Have you ever wondered why regardless of how hard you try to make things work out in your life; it never seems to happen?

Do you find that relationships seldom work out like you imagined they could and should?

Do you secretly struggle with obsessive thoughts and feelings of failure, despair, depression, fear, hopelessness and frustration?

Do you believe people do not like you, prefer not to be around you, or perhaps that your family would be better off without you?

Are your emotions and behaviour regulated by circumstances or a need for people to accept and approve of you?

As the youngest of four siblings from a highly stressful and unstable childhood, I struggled most of my life with self-sabotaging emotions and invasive thoughts as so many of us do from time to time.

I discovered, during decades of global ministry with families, children and adults, that many of us unconsciously suffer from past hurts and from the power that our childhood still holds over our lives.

†Believe me when I tell you, I understand what adults often face in life after emerging from the ashes and ruins of an unstable, and perhaps self-destructive, childhood.

†Few of us are able to connect the dots to realize that our daily psychological and emotional struggles have their roots in our childhood.

†I can assure you, we do not just walk away from unstable childhoods without some aspect of it, in later years, rupturing into our lives, even as Christians.

†Emotionally-charged family environments possess the potential of producing future adult instabilities without our awareness. Like a hidden polluted underground reservoir, it is capable of bubbling-up and impacting our lives regardless of how much denial we may try to hide behind.

I still remember the pervasive fear and anxiety that enslaved me while growing-up. As a little boy, I never knew what to expect next; therefore, my health, my roller-coaster emotions, and my chronic insecurities continued to invade my being as a child and later spilled-over into my adult life.

†Unstable home environments often require a child to be vigilant, alert, and always emotionally prepared for the unexpected crisis to occur. Many children, who emerge from such environments, become angry and emotionally-charged adults who need to control their environments and many of the people in them.

This type of **eggshell environment** becomes the foundation upon which a child will attempt to build his, or her, adult life. Childhood hurts and instability eventually interrupt the ability to grow-up feeling secure enough to love, be loved, and to feel valued.

My childhood included erupting altercations between my parents after they returned home from an evening of drinking in the neighbourhood bar.

I can still visualize that little boy hiding under his bed, crying, paralysed with fear, covering his ears to muffle his mother's pleas not to be hit again.

An untold number of adults emerge from similar childhoods. As adults, they will attempt to merge into the adult stream of life trying desperately to establish and maintain some illusive semblance of a productive and healthy life.

†Most of these adults will never understand why they cannot live and be happy like other people. Many will ultimately end-up blaming themselves. They often attempt to mimic the happy lifestyles of others because they deeply need to believe their past is behind them.

Most of this subversive **self-sabotaging** will emerge from subconscious childhood trauma and its associated insecurities. These invaders will springboard off past childhood traumatic experiences into our present lives to begin constructing their own unique cycle of emotional and behavioral instabilities.

†Our self-protective soul (our intellect, will, emotions) will attempt to insulate these intruders by sealing them off within a special section of our memory hotel in an effort to arrest and imprison these marauders.

This entire process is activated by an unquenchable desperation and need to be loved and accepted. Such a past infection of the soul will continually compete with any efforts to live happy and productive lives.

This self-sabotaging system will interfere with most attempts to develop a normal and stable life. In fact, it will continue to attack, much like an camouflaged sharp-shooter, by attempting to ambush our lives at any given opportunity.

†Our soul will attempt to deal with these intruding past hurts and instabilities by developing a subversive denial system. **Rationalization** and **denial** are twins; together they attempt to convince us that our childhood was not so bad after all. As part of this coverup, our mind will attempt to seal-off most memories of a tragic childhood.

†Our mind often attempts to do this because the alternative of facing the realization about our childhood could hurt much too deeply; especially with its companion beliefs that we were not good enough for our parents to love us.

This erosion may eventually bleed into our spiritual life and convince us that even God does not love us and he has abandoned us as well.

†Somewhere along life's journey, many of us will make an **inner vow** to never again allow anyone to hurt us. Consequently, a subversive program of isolation and distrust may develop that will hinder developing intimacy with others and with God.

These **self-affirmations** often activate a false assurance that we will never allow our past hurts and heartache to become our present. We do so without realizing it is already happening.

The Human Tendency To Numb

"Cast your burden on the Lord, and he will sustain you, He will never permit the righteous to be moved!" (Psalm 55:22)

Self-medicating, in today's world, has reached epidemic proportions and it is the preferred way to deal with stress and fears, regardless of the source.

Millions of suffering people either consciously, or unconsciously, chose to incorporate some form of a **numbing regimen** into their lifestyle to insulate against our twenty-first century's hectic lifestyle along with its companion travelers emotional, psychological and physical suffering.

Even when our lives, marriages, and families seem solid and fulfilling, we may still sense there is something missing so we will ultimately begin some ritual of numbing.

We seem aware that somewhere within, cloaked deep within the shadows of our soul, lies something lurking, awaiting its time of release. We sense it is a threat to our present and future happiness.

The human soul is armed with life-sabotaging memories, those emotional and psychological missiles that leave a trail of loneliness, sadness, despair, depression, hopelessness, and a reoccurring dissatisfaction with our life; it awaits the time of countdown to launch into our present, but why?

It all seems to escape rational reasoning and continues to defy any logical explanation. Many of us simply do not have collaborating memories of any past atrocities; however, we dare not probe to deep lest we discover them.

†Therefore, self-medicating is the preferred method to avoid pending pain, whether with alcohol, drugs, a marathon of television shows, sexual fantasies, or some other form of addictive stress relief. It has become North America's escape of choice to insulate against the gnawing and relentless pain of past and present hurts lying just below the surface building towards eventual eruption.

†For many of us, self-sabotaging emotions and behavior were most likely installed during childhood. Eventually, painful memories may begin to progressively seep into our conscious awareness and generate emotional, psychological, spiritual and physical distress.

Most of us start out in life with goals and dreams for our future. If we are aware of some of our childhood haunts, we most likely will make a determined effort to place them behind us and ignore the warning signals they emit throughout our lives.

A great deal of research and studies support the probability that the past will most likely resurface in varying degrees in our adult lives.

The **emotional whiplash** from an unstable childhood may become apparent through unexplained bouts with depression, sadness, feelings of hopelessness, despair, fear, and even self-mutilation like cutting, binging and purging.

Even an attempt to end our life reflects the depth of inner pain and turmoil that so many today are experiencing. Unexplainable inconsistent behaviour is often a warning sign that a deeper destabilizing eruption is mounting within.

✝So, we need to take a candid look into this twenty-first century cancerous epidemic. Traditional Christianity has launched its own counterattack in many churches. Biblical half-truths have been released among the global Christian community suggesting once we are experience the rebirth, we will no longer be impacted by past hurts.

> " ... and from among your own selves will arise men speaking twisted things, to draw away the disciples after them." (Acts 20)

Simply stated, this truth distortion implies that our past hurts, hardships, abuse and trauma will no longer impact us once we become a born-again Christian.

✝However, this is only a partial truth and it removes the responsibility of the convert to exercise the **power of choice** as required in scripture.

Scripture requires **dying-to-self** daily and **complete submission** to the Lord will in every aspect of our lives if we desire to obtain victory over past and present strongholds.

✝This process of **holistic cleansing** will progress in proportion to our intentional application of this biblical principle of dying-to-self.

This transformational process will necessitate the continuous ministry of the Holy Spirit in our lives (Galatians 5).

It is absolutely necessary that this process be continuous and it must be remembered its success is dependent upon our cooperative effort with the Holy Spirit. This condition is seldom talked about in church assemblies and less taught to new converts.

There are two aspects of the rebirth experience that must be activated and applied. If these two principles are not applied, the promise of victory will not become a reality in the convert's life, nor in the Christian's life.

The first aspect of the rebirth experience is revealed by Jesus in his discussion with one of the leaders of the Jews named Nicodemus.

"I assure you, most solemnly I tell you, that unless a person is born again, anew, he cannot ever see God." (John 3)

This is the initial and essential first-step that must take place to secure eternal life through Christ Jesus. Notice Jesus did not mention anything about church affiliation, membership, good works, or walking the aisle as a profession of faith.

The enemy has targeted this scripture, and others like it, because he is determined to detour as many as possible away from the rebirth. He has provided multiple placebos, substitutes, that look like, sound like, and even appear to be the real thing; however, they are merely decoys to distract from real thing.

Our birth-person, or the carnal part of us as the Apostle Paul refers to it, loves this buffet of religious options and has little problem with getting involved in some superficial aspect of religious activity; however, our human nature will not submit to the real thing as revealed in John, chapter three.

The second aspect of the rebirth experience is equally essential. It requires a daily process of surrender to the revealed will of God and dying-to-self through obedience.

Herein, is where we encounter the roadblock that detours many well-intentioned converts on their pursuit of healing from past hurts and failures.

"Walk and live, habitually in the Spirit, then, you will certainly not gratify the desires of the flesh." (Galatians 5, Amplified)

One of the most potent and deceptive weapons of the enemy has been and still is religion. In Genesis, chapters 1-3, we are introduced to the reason why.

Adam, in his original state, was created for intimacy and fellowship with his Creator. It was not something he did, but **who he was** in his natural created state.

This is why the Creator was able to walk in the cool of the day and talk with Adam. Our finite minds cannot fathom such a relationship with our Creator and our twenty-first century concept of worship and relationship is primitive and fleshly in comparison with this model.

I struggle to grasp what it must have been like for Adam to commune daily with his Creator and to intimately share with the all-powerful I AM.

Adam did not know anything about religion. There did not exist any formatted ceremonies, church attendance requirements, religious rituals, church memberships, sermons, business meetings, etc.

Adam was the only human who enjoyed pure, divine, and unmarred intimacy with his Creator.

Imagine, a life without rape, murder, greed, jealousy, deception, divorce, poverty, fear, emotional instability, disease, suffering, wars, abuse and trauma.

Once again, our minds cannot wrap around such a world because we have no frame of reference from which to make such a comparison.

Certainly our understanding of such a world is very limited, a world filled with God's presence. This quality of divine fellowship and intimacy is beyond our limited experiential knowledge for us to begin to comprehend.

This is the promise of our Creator and heavenly Father for **whosoever will** partake of the Lord's life-transforming rebirth. However, for now, our lives on earth must experience and reflect a progressive metamorphosis, much like that of the caterpillar prior to becoming a beautiful butterfly.

Only though the cooperative and progressive daily process of a **dying-to-self transformation** will this divine promise become our reality!

2

IS YOUR PERCEPTION YOUR REALITY?

> "What we see, smell, hear, taste, and feel are merely the gatekeepers to the mind's reconstruction of reality."
> (Richard Cytowie, M.D.)

Have you ever given thought to why you believe what you do? Are you aware that much of what you feel and how you behave are significantly influenced by your childhood experiences and the beliefs you develop during this period?

We often find comfort in believing we have selected the perfect career and are pursuing the best lifestyle. However, rarely do we realize many of our choices are significantly influenced by our past experiences (mindsets).

✝So, may I ask you this question. What do you think influences your decisions today? Of course, there are many varying factors that might be suggested; however, two consistent factors that do impact our life decisions are **perception** and our **interpretation** of life's events.

So, it is important for us to review this thing called perception to better understand what it is and how it may have enslaved our lives.

Here is a working definition of the term perception;
"Perception is the way we interpret the world around us."

✝Our perception of the world, of our family, of people, and especially of God were culturally molded earlier in our lives, especially during childhood.

✝Consequently, as adults we unconsciously interact with our environment based upon these unique memories, developmental beliefs, and experiences; however incorrect these perceptions and beliefs might be.

Here is a true-life situation that reflects the possible level of suffering our childhood may cause later in life.

(All personal similarities were altered to protect those they *represent*)

"Well, Mr. Stone, it is rare indeed that a man will darken the door of a counselor's office, much less request an appointment. I certainly admire your determination sir!"

"Truth be known doc, I am not determined at all. It is just that I am currently at a dead-end regarding a relationship in which I am currently involved. I figure it can't hurt to get another objective viewpoint."

"Oh, well then, please tell me more?"

"It is simply this; whenever I become involved in a personal relationship, I seem to keep running into the same wall! The ladies continually complain that I am not affectionate enough."

"Well, do you have any idea why they say that?"

"No sir, I have absolutely no idea! I take them out to nice places to eat and sometimes to a movie. Why, I even go with them shopping at times, if they ask! Now, you tell me doc, honestly now, does that sound like I am aloof and non-affectionate?

Why, sometimes I even fix things around their homes if there is a need, and I don't expect anything in return. I tend to think they should appreciate dating a gentleman for a change, one who is not making improper advances, trying to kiss them, or other things like that."

"Mr. Stone, it seems you present a good rebuttal to their complaints. Can you tell me a little about what it was like when you were growing up?"

"Well doc, I can tell you this about my parents. My father worked very hard and I never saw him do anything improper with my mother.

Why, they often talked and watched television together and they made sure the children had everything they needed. Yes sir, they were good moral parents!

In fact, they had their own separate chairs in the living room and were more like good friends most of the time, rather than husband and wife. I admired how my dad respected and treated my mom, you know like a lady, and he was not always trying to kiss her and other stuff like that. Yes sir, he showed her respect as a lady!

Why I can't remember ever seeing them hug, kiss, or even play around with each other, if you know what I mean. No sir, they surely respected and loved one another alright!"

In the case study I have placed before you, I believe it is apparent Mr. Stone has developed into adulthood with several perceived assumptions regarding intimacy and with an inadequate interpretation of his parents' behaviour and interactions.

†This case-study demonstrates how we, as children, may misinterpret our parents' behaviour and interactions. Childhood perceptions may eventually evolve into **core beliefs** that later impact our emotional and behavioural reactions as adults.

†Mr. Stone's cognitive reasoning skills were still developing during the formation of his perceptions regarding parental interactions; therefore, much of what he saw, heard, and experienced were not correctly processed.

Unfortunately, due to a child's lack of maturity and limited life experiences, his perception of family life and daily interactions are more concrete and have very little interpretative attachments.

†It is our **cultural perceptions** that will impact the development of what we eventually believe. This, in turn, will ultimately influence how we interact with friends, family and our environment in later years.

As adults, we will pursue what we believe is real and significant. However, our childhood distortions, along with their faulty perceptions, may erode our sense of reality in varying degrees.

†This adult pursuit may amount to little more than pursuing a mirage, an illusion. Why? Well, primarily because our interactions, decisions, and goals are based upon our interpretation of past

beliefs and experiences. These may develop from a deep inner need to escape our own harsh realities.

For example, the belief that people may not like us possesses the life-shaping power to influence our future behaviour and emotional responses towards people, family and the world around us. This, in turn, may significantly impact the quality of our lives and the lives of those we care about and love.

May I ask you a very important question at this point? Is it possible your past childhood experiences and hurts are still dictating your life interactions and decisions today?

Why do I ask this question? I ask it because our inner need to feel accepted and approved often indicate the amount of childhood damage that has not properly healed.

Therefore, any effort we make towards emotional, psychological, or spiritual maturity may greatly hinder, even block, our ability to **walk in the Spirit of God** as promised in Galatians, chapter five.

I encourage you to stop reading at this point, lay your book aside, and take some time to seriously reflect on my question.

Perhaps it might help to write down the things you struggle with, or dislike, about your life and yourself. Don't be alarmed if you discover some of your past hurts are rupturing into your life today.

†Our next area of focus will reveal how the world around us has **culturally reshaped** what we believe, value, and even why we pursue specific things as priorities, including the way we view God.

†Allow me to close this portion of our journey with a gripping true-life event which may reflect how an unstable childhood possesses the power to rob us of future happiness and joy;

It was almost five and today's caseload seemed relentless for some reason. I was stuffing file folders, papers, and notes, from the day's sessions, into my briefcase in an effort to unclutter my desk before I left for the day. This was when my receptionist Mary buzzed me;

"I apologize for this late interruption. I know you are probably preparing to go home, but there is a lady standing here who insists that it is urgent she see you now." "Mary, did she tell you what that urgency might be?"

I asked her while still clearing my desk;

"No sir, she did not."

"Very well Mary, give me about five minutes and send her in."

Normally, I do not experience this type of thing, however, lately we have continuously been inundated with an unprecedented stream of walk-ins; some with very serious life-threatening issues.

In fact, the last walk-in ended up in the hospital because of an attempted suicide. I immediately reasoned I must see this lady and not risk such a possibility.

I closed the briefcase and quickly slid it under the desk. As I looked up to buzz Mary and tell her to send the lady in; much to my surprise there she stood in the doorway.

She appeared well dressed, her hair seemed recently styled, she wore fashionable makeup, and she had well-manicured and polished nails; things I immediately look for as part of a my visual assessment regarding important self-care matters.

If a person is not interested in caring for their personal appearance, this might indicate a deep identity crisis.

"Thank you for seeing me sir. I apologize for this unscheduled intrusion; however, it's just that I'm not sure this matter will keep until I can get an appointment with you,"

"What seems to be your matter of urgency, if I may ask?",

I replied while reaching for my notepad and pen.

"And by the way may I have your name please?"

"There is no need for names. I won't be here that long, I assure you. You see, the matter before you is quite simple. Yes, it is very simple indeed!

It is just that I am very tired of the constant squabbles and accusations, telling me over and over what a complete loser and failure I have been all my life."

While speaking to me, her posture began morphing into a slump, no, rather more of a lump, while slithering down into her seat as she spoke.

Her eye contact was no longer direct, and her stately posture transitioned into that of a punished child while trying *to squeeze into a tiny ball.*

"Who is telling you such things? Is it your husband, your family, co-workers or someone else?"

Her silence and actions were quite troubling, to say the least.

"Look, if you want me to help you, it would be helpful if you were a little more forthcoming with some information."

Almost immediately, she straightened up, sat up very erect and, once again looked directly into my eyes. As she rearranged her shuffled clothes, seemingly with some embarrassment, she leaned forward and rested her elbows on my desk directly before me.

"Why, the voices in my head, doc, they always tell me what a loser I am! My thoughts are relentlessly telling me what a waste of space I am, how no one likes me or wants me around, what a complete failure I have been all my life and that I always will be a failure."

She sighed with a deep breath while leaning even closer, *"Now sir, is that being forthcoming enough for you?"*

I must admit I was caught completely off-guard by such a candid and refreshingly direct response;

"Thank you! Now, as we move forward this will be much better for both of us, I assure you! Now, why would you believe you are a failure, and that nobody wants you around? Has anyone ever told you this?"

Again, she shrank even deeper into her chair and, once more, reverted into a fetal position as if to protect herself.

Then, a soft muffled voice began to speak from the huddled mass of the woman who completely curled up in the corner of the chair one more.

"I never do anything that pleases mother, never! No matter how hard I try, it just isn't good enough for her. One night, when she thought I was in

bed asleep, I was standing on the stairs trying to muster-up enough nerve to go into the kitchen for a drink of water. That's when I heard her say it. She was talking with someone on the phone and she told them I was one major disappointment after another. Why can't my mommy love me?"

After a brief dialogue with this younger sounding part of her, I discovered that while a child she suffered a great deal of verbal abuse from her father and her mother was aloof much of her childhood years.

Most of her adult life was a cycle of one failed marriage after another. She appeared to be continually struggling with feelings of being unwanted and rejected by others.

Even her current relationship with her grown children remained strained and distant.

I need to direct your attention to the question which I asked earlier; whether you believe your past childhood can impact your adult life today.

†Do you think an adult woman, like the one I just described, is struggling with past hurts and rejection? Of course she was!

I feel confident most counsellors and pastors can identify with similar situations like this one. I believe it is imperative to remember our childhood is often entwined in our adult life;

"The past is not the past as long as it remains your present!"

3

THE POWER OF YOUR CHILDHOOD

> "For better or for worse, every living adult has lived through their childhood. More often than not, the quality of one's childhood impacts their adult life, relationships, mental health, and how they see the world. One of the most devastating impacts of childhood trauma is on self-image. the most devastating impacts of childhood trauma is on self-image."
> (Psychology Today)

The single most important influence in a child's development will be the family environment. The bonding provided within the home, or lack thereof, will either nurture and protect the child physically, psychologically, spiritually, and emotionally, or launch the child into the future with a life-long foundation for self-sabotage.

> *"Train up a child in the way he should go when he is old he will not depart from it." (Proverbs 22)*

Before we proceed, we need to take a closer look at this important portion of scripture which frequently is used to guarantee a child will grow-up into a godly adult and live accordingly.

The insertion of the word **should** during translation is unfortunate because it leads the reader to believe God is saying this is an unconditional guarantee that it will occur.

Many well-intentioned parents use this scripture to build their future hopes on for their child's life: however, future disappointment, heartbreak and confusion regarding God and his faithfulness to uphold his Word occurs when the child remains wayward.

Even a casual stroll through Old Testament history will reveal this such a guarantee is just not the case. Abraham was afraid the king of Gerar, when he beheld Sarah's beauty would want her; therefore, he might kill him if he knew Sarah was his wife. So, Abraham lied! He told the king Sarah was his sister.

David is the only man, mentioned in the entire Bible who we are told was **a man after God's heart** (Acts 13:22). However, it only takes a few minutes to review David's life and realize that as the King over Israel he was guilty of premediated murder, adultery, and numerous other sins.

Solomon, David's son and also the King over Israel, was greatly blessed by God, but he likewise committed gross sins before God including idolatry.

We could continue down the generational bloodline and will realize many of God's servants, often royalty and hand-picked by God, turned away from God and indulged in many sensual sins of the flesh.

†What is my point? Obviously, being one of God's children will not prohibit our self-centered life-choices and accountability for our ungodly decisions and lifestyle.

Unfortunately, denial presses multitudes of parents to rationalize this scripture and insist on believing this teaching assures them of their child's return to the Lord in later years.

†Parents crave assurance regarding their child's eternal welfare. Consequently, if their child attended church while growing-up, they will stand firm that these behaviors are proof their child was born-again and will return to the Lord regardless of poor choices in life.

The **power of denial** is one of our soul's attempts to assure us all is well with our life and the lives of our children. **Reality** becomes merely an illusion that is prefabricated deep within the laboratory of the human soul.

What About the Power of Choice?

"Choose this day whom you will serve .." (Joshua 22)

We must remember to interpret scripture with the understanding we are given the power of choice; always bear this in mind. God will not override our freedom of choice, even if it means it will ultimately lead to our own self-destruction!

The Importance of the Environment

"Let all you do be done in love." (1 Corinthians 16)

During the 1980's, I served as an agent in the child protection division in one of Florida's (HRS) family service centers.

The massive amount of child abuse and neglect these dedicated agents and workers witness daily was horrifying, to say the least.

- 1 in 4 girls and 1 in 6 boys will be sexually abused before they become 18 years old.

- Many of those, who are sexually abuse children, will be family members.

Are these statistics shocking? Although, not every child who emerges from an insecure and unstable environment will encounter major emotional issues as an adult, untold numbers will, and it will usually be without an understanding why?

The home is a child's launching pad into the future. The caregivers, albeit parents or others, will have the first opportunity at assisting the child towards a productive and healthy opportunity in life, or they will send them out into the world equipped with an unconscious **self-sabotaging soul program**.

The home environment is a critical and strategic factor in a child's future. The quality of the home's environmental nurturing will prepare the pathway for the child's future to a large degree.

Let's look at what is considered to be the basics needed to launch a child's future toward a positive and productive adult life;

The Ingredients Makes The Cake

- Unconditional love

- Self-confidence and high self-esteem

- The opportunity for productive peer interaction

- A Christian Holy Spirit-guided parental atmosphere

- A safe and secure home environment

- A biblically-framed parental guidance and discipline model.

With many years of experience as an educational specialist, who worked with disabled children in both public and private school settings, I witnessed many children who were products of an unstable home environment.

Over many years of teaching, I had ample opportunity to personally witness the impact and effects of both the stable and unstable home environments.

A conservative summary of my observations would be that the emotional impact of each type of home environment was very apparent whenever witnessing the child's daily interaction with both peers and adult authority figures.

Children who emerge from unstable homes seem to have a short emotional fuse. These children generally possess average, or above average, intelligence; however, they often demonstrate destructive emotions like anger and bullying, or insecurity and withdrawal.

They often have a very limited tolerance for any child who will not play, or act, in accordance with how they needed them too.

They usually **perceive** the behavior and interactions of others in an incorrect manner which often activated an inappropriate behavioral response towards them.

Characteristic emotions and behaviors of childhood trauma often include defensiveness, insecurity, anger, a poor self-image, avoidance, spontaneous emotional and physical outbursts.

Over time, I had the opportunity to meet and become better acquainted with many of the parents of these children.

Many of these parents were average, hardworking people with good parenting skills; however, there were also parents who were overwhelmed by life's demands and who often were single parents who simply were trying to survive in a world of constant demands, challenges and deadlines.

However, having said this, a considerable number of these families were indeed unstable in one way or another. Parenting appeared to be the least of their survival concerns.

Before we leave this aspect of our journey, it is very important for us to briefly discuss some of the primary characteristics of an unstable home environment as well.

It is important to point out that many of these children had nice comfortable home environments. It is not really so much about the physical setting of the home, although this is of course important; rather, the real stability, or instability, emanates from the loving and supportive interactions of the primary caregivers.

Characteristics of an Unstable Home

The type of home environments that rate at the top of the list are;

- An eggshell and unpredictable environment
- Unpredictable aggressive, emotional and behavioral responses from caregivers
- Physical, emotional, verbal, psychological and spiritual abuse
- Addictions - drugs, alcohol, sexual, eating, etc.
- Neglect and abandonment
- Mind manipulation games and inconsistencies
- Caregivers with unresolved psychological, emotional, and spiritual instabilities from their own childhoods

Insecurity and Acceptance

Children, by nature, require a predictable environment in which to grow. They require the assurance they are loved and unconditionally accepted no matter what their behavior may be.

So often, parents do not realize how they fall into cultural traps by comparing their children with one another.

I remember, as a young child, standing on a street corner with my mother while she talked with an acquaintance.

The subject of children came up and she proudly began to recount from the oldest to the youngest, which I was, what each child was successfully doing. One was in the police force, she said with a proud smile.

Then, there was the daughter who was in nursing training, and, of course, the next to the oldest son, was entering high school and making excellent grades. Why he probably would go to college, she bragged.

Finally, she got to me who was hanging onto her dress half-way hiding behind it;

"Larry here, well, he is just a happy-go-lucky child!"

What she meant by that statement and how I perceived it were probably very different, yet, here I am at seventy-three years old recounting this event to you.

Children require security, unconditional love, guidance, parental modeling, loving discipline, and above all else, parents who truly love and reflect Jesus Christ through their daily lives.

-4-
THE IMPACT OF THE HOME ENVIRONMENT

> "A child's early home environment has a profound effect on
> his well-being,. beginning in infancy"
> (Journal of Child Psychology and Psychiatry)

When Jesus was rejected as the only true source for reconnecting to the Creator, the human soul began developing a bias, a preference, towards following the flesh nature as the Apostle Paul refers to it.

This default bias is a religious substitution better known as **self-worship**. So, what exactly do I mean by the term religious?

A simple explanation of religion is a set of beliefs that channel human behavior through a predetermined system of cultural religious customs and ecclesiastical laws.

These cultural customs and laws mold our thinking into a specific mindset that influence, control, and manipulate our emotions, beliefs and ultimately our behavior.

In America, the concept of God is eroding to the level of representing whatever is comfortable for an individual's personal preference and lifestyle.

After spending decades working with people who were enslaved by religious traditions, it became very apparent that Christians also struggle with crumbling lifestyles.

They do not realize the damage that can be caused by this popular teaching which is interpreted to mean God assures us once we become a Christian, our past hurts and issues will no longer impact our present lives.

Many tend to accept this popular religious teaching that God automatically sweeps the impact of past mistakes and hurts under his forgiveness of our sins through Jesus once we become born-again.

"The past is only the past when it is no longer your present."

I invite you to now join me during an actual counseling session that represents this prevalent truth distortion among the Christian community regarding the power and impact of our childhood.

This counseling session occurred while I was a young pastor and counselor at a rural Canadian church. Let's now join the session;

"Thank you for seeing me pastor on such short notice. I realize you are very busy and have greater needs to serve than what I am bringing before you."

"Not at all Mrs. Crutchfield (the name is fictitious). If I can help you in any way, of course I want to do so. After all, is that not God's will to wipe away our tears and restore his joy and peace within us that he has so graciously provided for our lives through salvation?"

She immediately began to sob and it took her several minutes and a pile of Kleenex before she could compose herself.

"That's just it, pastor! I have never, ever experienced that kind of joy and peace, never! I am nothing but a fraud. You might as well know it right now!

Like so many of my church friends, I come to church, fake a smile, engage in some small talk, use the religious lingo of 'God bless you and I love you sister', then at the end of service, I return home to the same prison I have lived in forty years. Nothing, I tell you, absolutely nothing, ever changes pastor. So, please tell me pastor, where is God in all this?"

It was very apparent that Mrs. Crutchfield was very distraught. What really bothered me was she and her husband are founding pillars in our church and have been for more than forty years.

"Why don't you begin by telling me what exactly is going on in your life? It can't be all that bad, can it? After all, you have touched so many lives in this church through providing dinners to the sick and visiting the our hospital shut-ins.

In fact, I recall you taught some successful, and I might add, capacity-filled Bible classes about how to obtain victory in Jesus.

You know, Mrs. Crutchfield, we all have seasons in our lives when we feel we have let God down, or for some unknown reason, he is very distant.

I feel confident that you are going through one of these periods in your life and we, as a church, will certainly do whatever we can to help you!"

She immediately squared her shoulders, sat very upright with a rather stern look on her face while placing her hands together in her lap.

"Look Pastor, I am going to level with you. I know you mean well. I do appreciate that, but I am afraid you are just very much out of touch with what is really going on among the people here.

I suspect after my visit you will ask that I leave the church, I of course will oblige your request; however, it is time for you to be introduced to the real world situation that exists within this church. In fact, I suspect it exist in most other churches as well.

I have friends and acquaintances in many church denominations, and many of them are just like me, I am sorry to say pastor! Yep, just like me! They too are a big fraud who find it necessary to play the part of a nice happy church member!"

I tried to reassure her, but she immediately gestured with her hand not too. She sat very erect, in fact it appeared by her posture she might be ready to deliver a sermon. I became quite uneasy about what to expect next from this point on.

"Pastor, for example, I am an alcoholic and I have been one for most of my adult life. My husband beats me, every now and then, just to make himself feel manly, I guess. Then, he goes out with the boys and I don't usually see him for days at a time.

My little boy has been found wondering the neighborhood streets unattended and the neighbors find him and kindly keep him for me until I am able to sober-up after a week or two of a drinking binge.

Do you need me to continue pastor? I can tell you more because there is so much more to tell?"

"But Mrs. Crutchfield, let me just say I have known you and your husband for many years. I have seen your hearts reach out to so many people in this community.

Why, the people you represent yourself and your husband to be are quite hard to for me to swallow. If you and your family are experiencing such hard times why haven't you reached out to the church body?"

"Help me", she interrupted? *"I have been an active member of this church for more than forty years. You, nor the church leadership, have never had an inkling about my deplorable situation, much less be aware of the defeated and devastating lives in this church!"*

She abruptly stood up, moved away from her seat while quickly gathering her things. She started hurriedly walking towards the door, abruptly turned around, walked hastily back, leaned over my desk while staring directly at me;

"Pastor, you are a kind man and I do appreciate your good intentions. However, like many other pastors in this community, your world is insulated in your ivory tower lifestyle from the real world of the people you profess to represent and understand.

Your church business and finance meetings, summer youth camps, Christmas parties, family outings and the other activities going on do not begin to touch the horrific suffering of the people in this church!

I mean you no insult, kind sir, but even your fine sermons about God's love, forgiveness, and how there is victory in Jesus have not been able to touch our wretched family situation all these years, nor have they impacted many others from what I hear and see.

Have you ever asked yourself why? Well, perhaps it is time to do so! After my departure, please make it a priority to do so; yes, please allow me to urge you to do so!

What broken people, like my husband and I, need is a Saviour who can practically and effectively show us how to find the root of our wretched lifestyles! Then, we need help learning how to receive healing; not some religious band-aide of another sermon on love and forgiveness, or a handshake and pat on the back as we leave!

My dear pastor, kind sir, there exists an absolute crisis within the churches today, in this church, and the people who sit weekly before their pastors are drowning in their own heartache and suffering right before their pastors and church leaders". Good evening sir!

Then, just as suddenly as she appeared, she vanished, out into the torrential storm leaving her gentle kiss on my forehead as a pivotal and life-changing marker I shall never forget!

Unfortunately, this powerful dialogue represents the silent majority of Christians who attend many of our churches today.

Please allow me to provide another brief example, if I may, regarding this crisis that is unfolding within many of our churches worldwide.

I remember how deeply touched I became after reading a book regarding the impact of an unstable childhood on an adult life.

I decided to accept the author's challenge and complete his online psychological survey to determine how much of my own adult life had healed since my childhood.

I was quite confident the results would reflect I had significantly healed from my own traumatic childhood experiences.

However, much to my surprise and shock, the survey indicated quite the contrary. In fact, it revealed I was still approximately eighty-five percent unhealed.

Even with all my theological training, global trauma work, and years of Christian counseling and ministry in various denominational church settings, I remained an unstable adult! I unknowingly hid behind unconscious **denial** and **rationalization** over the years like so many do.

†Such unstable childhoods simply do not vanish regardless of how much you and I might want to believe they do. No amount of denial and emotional medicating will change the residual impact from unresolved wounds and scars during childhood.

†Our soul usually develops a complex denial system, during our childhood years, to mask our pain and fears that are the result of horrific suffering.

Unfortunately, Christians have accepted the half-truths of the enemy that once we become Christians, the past can no longer impact our lives.

The enemy will use well-intentioned people, pastors, counsellors, educators and parents to unconsciously propagate these distorted scriptural teachings from the Bible.

†A primary cause of this poisonous approach to the blessings of being born-again is a lack of understanding and awareness of the potent power of the **carnal nature** within our human composition.

Let's continue now and look deeper into the power of our childhood regarding this matter, shall we?

-5-
WHICH COMES FIRST -
THE CHICKEN OR THE EGG?

"The goal of good parenting is to help children mature in
wisdom and moral judgments in the context of a disciplined and
holy lifestyle. Effective parenting structures a child's environment
to encourage maturity in every sphere of the child's life."
(Sherry Allchin-Christian Counselor)

Becoming a Christian does not automatically heal our past
hurts and wounds. **Personal application** is required through the
wisdom of the Holy Spirit.

He will lead and guide us along life's healing journey if we
continue to develop intimacy and pursue his will for our life.

Often, scriptures are lifted out of context to support an
individual's need for security and comfort. What happens so
often is we tend to read into scripture our personal bias, rather
than, allow the scripture to speak to us as the Spirit enhances our
understanding.

Proof texts, as this process is referred to, was a very popular
teaching method in many Bible schools, churches, and
seminaries. It was once widely acclaimed as an excellent method
of preaching and teaching; however, overtime the abuse of this
approach has placed this method under scrutiny.

It is the process of selecting one, or more verses, and
expounding on them out of their original surrounding context in
the scripture. By this method, the original intent of the scripture
can be lost or easily manipulated to say something it does not
mean.

If we are to be effectively used by God to assist in the intricate process of **inner healing**, we must do as the ancient adage suggests; **put the horse before the cart**.

†Only those who are walking in the Spirit of the living God are in a position for God's **holistic healing** to pour into them and through them.

†Past hurts and troubling experiences often remain buried deep within the memories of the human soul (our emotions, will and intellect).

†These memories may eventually be triggered by any sensory similarity with the original traumatic event that caused the original wound in the child.

One frequent symptom, which may emerge out of childhood trauma, is the need to control those around them, including the environment.

An inherent and unconscious need to control one's life, and the lives of those around them, often surfaces overtime. This unfortunate compulsion usually bleeds into an adult's life in varying stages.

†**Insecurity** activates an attempt to exert some measure of control over the environment. Why? Because the person may be overwhelmed with **obsessive thoughts** of being harmed, or other related fears that spiral from past situations.

I recall a past case in which a seven year old girl could not be trusted to climb into the lap of any male without acting out sexually with that male, even if the person was a family member. She had a past of repeated sexual abuse during her early developmental years; therefore, to her it was merely a method of expressing love.

†An invasion of our mind with thoughts of worry and anxiety will often generate some form of repetitive behavior. This occurs as a soul strategy to detour a persons focus off a repetitive thought of a past hurt.

†By attempting to control some of the events in their environment, it generates a false sense of security for the

moment. It is an internal perception that develops over a period of years, usually from intense childhood suffering and pain.

Eventually, the need for security enslaves their thoughts and lives, as well as the lives of their love-ones, which in turn intensifies an emotional need for more control.

It becomes a vicious repetitive cycle and a very destructive one, not only for the person, but for the family as well. This subconscious cycle of obsessions and compulsive behaviours will ultimately intensify a person's stress and anxiety.

It tends to reinforce any **self-sabotaging cycle** of emotions and behaviour that evolve from their need to fill that they can predict the immediate future.

Very often, the need to justify one's strange behaviour becomes overwhelming. This in turn activates the need to justify their compulsive behaviour. **Self-rationalization**, **denial** and **justification** are then added to the enslaving cycle of bondage.

All of these are responses to perceived, or real threats. They tend to generate many unconscious and unstable personal beliefs that eventually become the building blocks of their personality.

The Bile uses the word **strongholds** to identify anything that maintains bondage in our lives even though we have been positionally set-free through the atonement of Christ Jesus.

In many cases, the mind will attempt to seal these troubling memories off as an attempt to protect the person; therefore, the person may not really know why they act as they do, only that it brings them a measure of mental relief.

Religion is likewise a compulsion. It satisfies the deep inner need to reconnect to the Creator, although it too is a detour designed by the enemy.

As Christians, we may start a religious pilgrimage towards pleasing God in accordance with specific cultural traditions and beliefs.

We may pursue whatever illusion of God we subconsciously find comfortable. We will focus on a particular attribute of God like love, peace, power, etc. that helps us feel loved and secure.

This religious journey begins to reflect either a re-enforcement, modification, or an complete abandonment of whatever we grew up to believe as a child regarding God, family, love, sex, and the world around us.

What I have just described is precisely the American illusion of God and how America's buffet of religious choices often complement our subconscious instabilities. Ultimately, it will impact our life pursuits and our eternal destiny.

So, what is wrong with this picture, you might ask? Well, for one thing, religion is not a true reconnection with God! Religion cannot provide real security, stability and joy. **Intellectual beliefs** about God, Jesus, Christianity, etc. are manufactured by-products of our soul's attempt to feel safe.

In order for the Bible to become a reality in our lives, the Holy Spirit must apply it to our souls. This necessitates a true, deep and life-changing transformation through the **rebirth process** (John 3) and a continual **dying-to-self**.

Once these two essentials ingredients are in place, then the process of surrender and walking in the Holy Spirit can become a reality in our lives. The Apostle Paul tells us that only through the daily process of submission and learning how to walk in the Spirit, can we experience true holistic healing and victory in life.

Which Comes First, the Chicken or the Egg?

This old proverbial question usually bothers people for some reason. It is what I refer to as a loop question. It is labeled this because it involves, to a large degree, circular reasoning which seemingly has no reasonable solution.

Life is very much like this loop. Our lives often seem to continue moving, but seldom does it bring true happiness, inner peace and joy.

During childhood, children receive foundation beliefs and behaviors from their parents. Unfortunately, in this century the accelerating decay of our culture and the epidemic spread of immorality have produced a whiplash of insecurity and fear.

If a child cannot feel loved, valued, and wanted during childhood, then, most likely the child's emotional and psychological development will become off-center.

Therefore, the belief system that will be set in place during childhood will greatly impact the child's adult life with an underlying fear of rejection and disapproval.

Self-centered parenting, which I am personally familiar with and guilty of in my own life, can activate significant self-sabotaging within family members, especially in the lives of the children.

Children who grow-up within an insecure home environment usually develop an unconscious self-protective mindset. This mindset, in turn, spins-off emotions and behaviors that are **self-protective** above all else.

These children do not have adequate developmental tools to properly assess and interact with their peers and with others in our culture and world.

The mission of Jesus was to set the captives free. The major focus has to be to set each of us free from ourselves!

"He has sent me to announce release to the captives, and recovery of the sight for the blind, to send forth as delivered to those who are oppressed, who are downtrodden, crushed and broken by calamity."
(Luke 4-Amplified)

ARE YOU AN EMOTIONAL STUFFER?

> However, what we learn in our society is not how to work with our emotions, but how to block and avoid them. We do it quite well: Between alcohol use, prescription drugs, screen time, there are a multitude of ways to avoid our feelings.
> (Hilary J. Hendel)

Another residual spinoff from an unstable childhood is the tendency to **suppress**, or stuff, **our feelings**.

Humans learn to unconsciously suppress past hurts as a survival mechanism to help manage their fears and painful emotions.

This is an unconscious strategy of our soul as an attempt to avoid our fears and pain from past hurts and disappointments. Nevertheless, our traumatic childhood haunts most likely will bleed over into our adult life.

†This unconscious process of avoiding pain is a powerful soul program and it potentially develops into a defensive response whenever we feel threatened, even if imagined.

†Most likely, these childhood coping mechanisms will resurface during our adult years. It is our soul's attempt to compare daily situations with those of our childhood trauma to avoid any perceived threats.

†It is an automatic security mechanism. However, this automatic security system does not always function well due to the built-in triggers from childhood that release a **false alarm** and activate them.

†Sensory stimulation (smell, taste, touch, hearing, visual) may automatically trigger this subconscious self-protective reaction that, in turn, activates an emotional and behavioural response that is not always appropriate.

These struggling adults, without realizing it, will store primary self-sabotaging beliefs in memory files that have attached default responses to a specific perceived or real threats.

Ultimately, these internal security alarms may develop into full-blown emotional and behavioural responses like anger, rage, violence or an attempt to escape from the perceived threat. The spectrum of possible irrational emotional and behavioural reactions are many.

†Most adults, who emerge from unstable childhoods, may insist their home environment was fine, when in reality it was not. For survival purposes they have convinced themselves they are telling the truth.

This too is part of the internal self-protective system; unfortunately, it often will inhibit, if not block, most attempts of therapeutic interventions

†Why? Because, as an automatic safeguard mechanism of the human soul, it will attempt to seal-off perceived hurtful memories within an **amnesic barrier.**

It will then store them out of the normal memory retrieval stream within a special memory section much like a library.

Unfortunately, this attempt to protect us is merely a band-aide, much like covering a bee-sting while leaving the stinger and poison deep within the wound.

†In order to survive perceived pain, the soul may then generate what is referred to as an **emotional numbing** intervention.

As adults, we learn to self-insulate against any uncomfortable situation by utilizing specific numbing alternatives; albeit drug, eating, watching television, lengthy periods at computer video games, etc.

Almost anything can become a **numbing**, or coping mechanism, utilized by conscious mind to escape unpleasant and uncomfortable circumstances.

†This process of unconscious escapism is so powerful it can actually pass a lie-detector test in certain situations without the adult having any conscious awareness of the real truth.

With so many subversive self-defense mechanisms operating in our lives, it often becomes impossible to maintain normal and healthy relationships with anyone, particularly with ourselves.

What must occur if wholeness is to be achieved? It is imperative that we reconnect the human spirit and soul via the rebirth. Then, it is imperative that we allow the Spirit to utilize whatever strategy deemed necessary to restore wholeness in our lives.

†However, a word of caution is needed here. The enemy has developed many coping mechanisms to detour us away from God's truth. They eventually lead to self-sabotage and ultimately will hurt those we love and care about.

Why is it important that we discover these inlaid self-destructive boobytraps? Because they are autonomic self-destructive elements of past pain and trauma that often rupture into our daily lives and, much like a cancer, will continually eat away at the fabric of our lives.

†Progressively, these intruders seep into our conscious awareness through one or more of our sensory processing systems (the five senses). They begin to generate instability in our lives, but we seldom have little, or no clue, why we are feeling or acting as we do.

On the next portion of our journey, we will discuss in greater detail how this process of our internal security system may become corrupted by trauma and evolve into becoming our worst enemy.

The Dangers of Suppressed Emotions

What are **suppressed emotions?** Simply stated, they are emotions to which we choose to ignore or respond. We do so either intentionally by attempting to ignore them, or they are subconsciously hidden by our soul's security system.

However, it is important to note our emotions may eventually bleed into our conscious awareness during our adult life. It will occur especially if past hurts are triggered by similar present-day circumstances that parallel the original trauma during childhood.

Emotions are not well understood even today. The potential physical, psychological and spiritual damage they may cause over a period of time is underestimated.

Most medical and scientific journals repeatedly warn us that self-destructive emotions like anger, rage, hate, fear, insecurity, stress, dread, despair, depression, etc., will progressively erode our total health while undermining our emotional stability.

"For being a man of two minds (doubting)

is unreliable and unstable about everything

he thinks, feels or decides."

(James 1, Amplified)

-7-
THE SUPREMACY OF THE SOUL

"As man (person) thinks, so is he." (Proverbs 23)

When the serpent, Satan, approached Eve in the garden, he was well aware of God's command not to eat from the tree of the Knowledge of Good and Evil.

This brief portion of scripture reveals a couple of very important points regarding our own daily struggles with the enemy.

"And Adam said, this is now bone of my bones, and flesh of my flesh. Therefore, shall man leave his father and mother and shall cleave unto his wife and they shall be one flesh." (Genesis 2: 21-25)

First of all, notice the serpent chose to deceive Eve, not Adam. He did not do so because she was the weaker of the two. Rather, it was because Eve had not received God's law directly; she received it second-hand through Adam.

What this clearly indicates, if we read the entire passage of Eve's creation, is she was co-equal with Adam and in a vital relational union with him.

The Bible says absolutely nothing to indicate Eve was inferior to Adam, not in intelligence nor in her relationship with God.

However, when Bible scholars, theologians, pastors and others begin to speculate, assume, and read into this creation picture; it is then the enemy has opportunity to distort and twist God's Word to implant deception and lies into the human soul.

Satan is a master at repackaging divine truth! He does so to present an appealing diversion. He desires that we not understand how our soul operates.

This is the part of the human composition which the apostle Paul refers to it as his **wretched man**, that part of us which naturally resists God and His divine will for our lives (Rom. 7).

Our Soul Person Has a Mind of its Own

"When we were living in the flesh (mere physical lives), the sinful passions that were awakened and aroused by what the law makes sin were constantly operating in our natural powers (bodily organs), in the sensitive appetites and wills of the flesh, so that we bore fruit for death." (Romans 7, Amplified)

The Apostle Paul continually makes reference to our daily warfare, the inner conflict, that all Christians must confront.

He further explains that this inner conflict is between our born-again spirit-person and our soul, or birth, person; the old flesh nature which we are born with.

Notice he refers to this **identity crisis** as a mere physical life in comparison with another life. Is this a primary concern of Paul? You bet it is and he takes considerable time to explain this on-going conflict for all of God's future disciples who likewise will be confronted by this ongoing warfare.

"We know that the law is spiritual; but I am a creature of the flesh, carnal and unspiritual, having been sold into slavery under the control of sin." (Romans 7)

We will need to examine this portion of scripture more closely to obtain a better understanding regarding this double-minded, two-directional, human composition with which we are born. Please read Romans, chapter 7, before proceeding further with me.

First of all, please note in this verse Paul acknowledges that he is a creature of the flesh, unspiritual, sold into slavery. Wow! Now this is quite a statement considering God greatly used him to help provide the foundation for Christianity.

In summary, what is being presented by Paul is the overwhelming truth that all humanity is sold into slavery and is in need of emancipation and redemption through Jesus Christ.

Another significant aspect of this brief passage of Scripture boldly states that all humans are under the control of sin. Sin, in its original context, means to miss the mark much like someone would miss the mark during target practice.

"We are not sinners because of what we do, rather, we do sinful things because we are sinners!"

It unfortunately has taken five decades for this author to realize how my adult life was still profoundly impacted by the ravages of my unstable childhood and how my wretched human nature still held much of my life in bondage.

The Apostle Paul declares that all humanity is likewise a slave to its natural and sensual appetites with all its inherent passions, desires, and faulty worldly reasoning.

✝This is why denial plays such a powerful role in our lives. Denial becomes an automatic installation when we emerge from unstable childhoods.

✝It attempts to buffer any future pain by masking and hiding the root cause of our present struggles. It strives to convince us that the hurts and bondage of our past never occurred and did not happen like we might think it did.

It is imperative for us to realize the enslaving truth about our childhood, especially if our adult lives are not reflecting tranquility and freedom from self-sabotaging emotions and behaviors.

Unfortunately, much of traditional Christian teaching misleads us to believe once we become Christians our past hurts and experiences will no longer have any major impact on our lives. It is presented to us as if it is an automatic download process, which it is not!

Although this teaching is accurate from a positional (theologically) aspect; nevertheless, on the experiential side (practical) side, it is a very deceptive, misleading, and an incomplete presentation of the rebirth process.

In itself, it places handcuffs on new Christian converts and on the Christian pilgrim, who continues to struggle daily with the natural aspect of the human composition whenever pursuing victory in Christ Jesus.

From what I have witnessed globally, this incomplete teaching establishes one of the strongest sources of today's epidemic falling away of Christians from an active pursuit of God.

These weary pilgrims slip into apathy, hopelessness, despair, chronic depression, and even an abandonment of God after many trails at living the Christian life.

This usually happens after receiving the rebirth. They triumphantly march into tomorrow armed with the false expectations of automatic victory in their lives.

Here are a few of the current teachings that often become a stumbling-block for God's people after life confronts them with constant setbacks and failures:

- Expecting immediate and automatic victory in Jesus over life's obstacles and storms

- Expecting the blessings of heaven to abundantly line their pathway throughout life

- Expecting minimal suffering and heartache in life

- Expecting automatic victory over Satan and his attacks

- Expecting automatic acceptance and love from God's people

- Expecting automatic victory over past bondages, addictions, hurts, emotional and behavioral issues

Tragically, such divisive twisting of scripture generates some form of alienation from a God.

During the lifetime of many Christian pilgrims, they unfortunately discover a very different situation within the traditional church scene in America and much of Europe.

The enemy uses this infiltration of biblical teaching as one of his many effective strategies to derail well-intentioned followers of Christ who ultimately become disillusioned and turn away from their pursuit of Jesus.

DO YOU STRUGGLE WITH CONTROL?

"Anything that makes us feel helpless, lacking fundamental control over our surroundings, can have a lasting impact, particularly if this happens when we are young."
(Glen Croston, Ph.D.)

Before Jesus entered the earthly realm, the Pharisees, Sadducees, and Sanhedrin were the ultimate authority figures over Israel.

Basically, whatever they said to the Jewish community became the law of the land and it usually had full support of the secular government.

God's people often resented the arrogance, power, and religious façade of their religious leaders; however, they had little choice but to submit.

Then Jesus arrived on the scene. Before long, his divine authority began to clash with that of the corrupt religious rulers and they determined to trap Jesus and kill him.

Jesus began to expose their many lies, deception and corruption. He even referred to them as whited sepulchers (a small area cut out space in a rock) full of dead-men's bones.

In other words, ,Jesus compared them to an eye-appealing white burial tomb which contained nothing more than the decayed remains of a dead person.

In today's world, those of us who have emerged from broken and unstable home environments usually struggle with self-sabotaging emotions regarding authority figures.

Most likely, during daily life, we will encounter a person who will say or do something that is similar to what someone did to us while a child; something that caused us pain.

This may in turn trigger a subconscious memory of someone, a parent, sibling, or uncle, who hurt us while a child. This may then trigger an inappropriate emotional response, after which we may be left embarrassed and perplexed about our bizarre behavior.

The paradoxical thing about this inner conflict with authority figures is that many children who struggle with authority figures often become adults who subconsciously become authority figures or are attracted to them.

Over decades of ministering with people with control conflicts, I witnessed many individuals who struggled with perceived or actual authority figures, I was one of these people.

These paradoxical conflicts unfortunately erode and sabotage many relationships including marriage. It is extremely difficult to survive in such a volatile relationship, albeit personal or professional.

†Why? Because those of us who experience early conflict with authority figures, do not only see these people as strong, but we also see them as threatening which generates emotional insecurity and self-destructive introspection. Eventually such relationships may develop into a love-hate conflict and a power struggle within the relationship.

†One of the ways insecure and fear-laden people attempt to deal with their insecurities is by attempting to control their environment and many of the people in it.

This inner need to control often generates a deep desire for order and perceived perfectionism. These behavioral obsessions may ultimately evolve into subconscious attempts to manage this emotional rollercoaster through extreme measures of personal and environmental controls.

†Adults, who emerge from homes in which someone was a primary controller, frequently will struggle with resentment and

anger and without any warning, it may erupt during a time of perceived insecurity.

In fact, if a person marries one who does attempt to control the relationship, that spouse may repress and stuff their own feelings to avoid conflict.

Unfortunately, if there are years of repression in a relationship, the repressed partner may become a mere shadow, a silent partner, a mere puppet without any voice in the relationship.

They will unconsciously associate the controlling situation with their childhood; therefore, they will attempt to repress their own insecurities, fears and anxiety.

When these adults attempt to build a personal or working relationship with such a person, they ultimately will resist their control either in a passive-aggressive manner or in open defiance.

†This loop relationship often results from growing-ups within a home environment with rigid expectations. If the primary caregiver regards the way that a child is performing a task as unsatisfactory, then the child may develop a core belief that **performance** is the only way to earn approval and love from others.

†The first authority figures the child most likely will encounter are usually those who are the primary caregivers and, of course, the child will desperately seek to earn their approval, virtually at any cost.

This performance-based belief system will eventually reinforce a belief and mindset that one must earn acceptance and love through performance.

Such an unstable relationship may ultimately evolve into subversively controlling the lives of the children as well; often without being consciously aware of it.

The Power Of The Soul

Allow me to share a very practical example from a past counseling situation, (the name and exact details have been altered) of a **fight or flight response** which I encountered numerous times early in my counseling ministry.

Mrs. Jeffrey was rolled into the office by a church friend. She was brought to me because of concerns regarding her declining will to live.

The lady was a senior, an invalid unable to get out of the chair on her own for several years. She required virtually round-the-clock supervision, but still lived in her apartment.

After an hour of introductory dialogue, I began to press towards the core issues of her declining will to live;

"Well, Mrs. Jeffrey, it seems you have avoided sharing much of your earlier life, including what your childhood. Can we do this now?"

She avoided direct eye contact and mumbled something about never feeling wanted, or loved, by her father. I began explaining how our mind attempts to insulate painful memories of past hurts so we can continue with our lives.

However, I pointed out, in many situations, this automatic mechanism of the mind does not properly work and eventually these memories begin to leak into the adult's conscious awareness.

"Mrs. Jeffrey, I need to ask you what you may perceive as a painful question to address. Why have you avoided telling me anything about your relationship with your father?

For the first time during our session, she looked up at me and stared intently into my eyes without a twitch. My associate and I also noted a decisive alteration in her facial features as well.

She sat-up rather erect with her hands no longer twitching; all of which are usually signs of stress and foreboding inner fears.

Even her caregiver took note of these changes and appeared puzzled, as if she had never seen these changes over years as her caregiver.

"Did your father harm you in any way or cause you to feel unloved?"

Suddenly, without warning, she jumped out of the chair, bolted out of the door, leaving three very started people unable to respond for a few minutes. Mrs. Jeffrey left her chair overturned on the floor before us.

Now, Mrs. Jeffrey possessed valid medical certification of her disability and she was physically incapable of getting out of the chair on her own. She had not walked, or moved out of the chair on her own for several years.

As we recovered from the shock, but before we could organize our thoughts sufficiently to search for her, she returned, barely able to hold herself up while leaning against the outside wall of the building.

After we helped her back into her chair and she regained some composure, she had no memory of the events. The power of the human soul and its intricate control over the human composition is beyond human comprehension!

Childhood - Foundation for Lifelong Beliefs

Even the manner in which an infant is handled and cared for will activate the installation of primary beliefs regarding acceptance and love.

This foundation system of core beliefs will ultimately resurface with various aspects of related emotions and behaviors.

They will likely bleed into the adult's life and possibly disrupt the normal flow of daily activities. Many children, who experienced a repeated degree of confrontation within the household environment will ultimately attempt to subconsciously control their own surroundings as an adult.

†Such powerful behavioral controls may become a significant component of the self-sabotaging profile as an adult.

Once again, we are reminded that our soul controls our emotions and behaviors. This scripture refers us back to the teaching of James regarding a *"double-minded man who will be unstable in all his ways"* (James 1).

This ancient behavioral and emotional principle is foundational to what we are told about parenting;

"Train up a child in the way he should go (in keeping with his individual gift or bent) and when he is old he will not depart from it." (Prov. 22)

†So often, as parents, we question the wisdom of this proverb without understanding that it is not based upon our best efforts as parents.

†Rather, it focuses on the strength of a childhood foundation that parents have the privilege and opportunity to establish during the child's formulative years.

†Parents must model a Christian lifestyle before their children daily. Their lives before their children will speak much louder than their verbal dialogues.

Parents must walk it out, not merely talk it out, if they desire to cement basic healthy core beliefs and emotions in their child.

Believe me, this author well understands the power of a self-destructive home environment. I not only lived it, but I also reproduced it.

†As past hurts and trauma erupt and rupture into our lives, be sure you seek the Holy Spirit's guidance and obtain competent counsel to avoid sabotaging not only your life, but the lives of those you care about and love.

-9-
ARE YOU A DECEIVED BELIEVER?

Let me set before you this proclamation, if I may;
"For they failed to understand the meaning of the miracle; for their hearts
had grown calloused and become dull."
(Mark 6)

Much of todays' Christianity possesses a veneer, a superficial covering, that appears to be faith; however, beneath this immediate appearance lies, for the most part, unbelief!

"If anyone is deficient of wisdom, let him ask of a giving God who gives to everyone liberally. Only, it must be in faith that we ask without doubting or wavering" (James 1)

†The foundation upon which we must live the Christian life is dependent upon our faith, an unwavering belief in God based upon his Word and not our private interpretation of it, nor our circumstances.

The enemy of our souls has infiltrated God's Word today and he has mastered the skill of misinterpreting God's Word in such a way that it enslaves our intellect and persuades us that we are indeed walking and living the faith life!

†**Deception** has always been one of Satan's greatest tools to detour Christians away from true faith. It worked on Eve and it still works today. Those who desire to live god-honoring lives often fall victim to this entrapment.

†However, our godless environment progressively reprograms our minds in a very subtle, but powerful way. One major way we have been deceived and manipulated is that we are indeed living our lives by faith. Our cultural mindset has been progressively reprogrammed to deceive millions to accept that they really

believe God's Word and walk by faith; however, in reality it is merely **intellectual agreement** that many claim is biblical faith.

I remember, as a small child in church, wondering why God never showed up during the church services. Oh, people walked the aisle to make a profession of faith and to confess they received Jesus as their Savior.

However, as I had opportunity to see some of these people at other times I became very confused by what I witnessed as a small boy.

In Bible studies, group gatherings, and other related Christian activities, it appears Christians are loving and caring.

However, over the years I became deeply discouraged, while a counselor and minister during later years, as I discovered Christians who professed to love the Lord and who claimed to be in pursuit of continual intimacy with Jesus were actually living a **double-standard** lifestyle outside of the church walls.

Their sterile and hypocritical lifestyles did not seem to bother them. Later, in my own life, I realized I too was a fraud, a fake, an imposter who was brainwashed into believing I was living the faith life.

Slowly, as I continually cried out to God for mercy and help, I began to develop an unquenchable thirst to walk in the same power as did the early church in the book of Acts.

However, for many years, I found it more comfortable to not swim up-stream against the traditional current of hypocritical religious beliefs and traditions.

The enemy knows the basic entrapments of our human predisposition. Deep from within there is a driving need to become one of the status quo and just do as the crowd does, just go with the flow.

†We deceptively begin to convince ourselves this is how to be liked and appreciated. It is a good thing Jesus did not decide to pursue this same avenue of complacency in his redemptive mission on earth.

Why not, at this point on our journey, listen-in to a conversation between two time-travelers, the same ones introduced in my book - <u>Rediscovering the Image of God for Your Life</u>?

†Our time-travelers are returning to the historic period prior to the crucifixion of Jesus. It will provide a great opportunity for us to look deeper into this matter of faith and how we should be living our lives for the glory of God in our own time-period.

So, strap your seatbelts on because here we go on our visit back into time to the days when Jesus was ministering. Let's hitch-a-ride with our time-travelers and listen to Jesus. Ready? Ok! Here we go!

"Well, here we are and I believe Jesus will be speaking today. Come along now, my dear companion. Here, this seems to be a good spot to sit down and wait for Jesus to pass by.

Now, here in this spot we should be able to observe him while he teaches. We should be able to hear what he has to say regarding how we can live the Christian life. Our generation certainly claims to have the last word on it, does it not?

Sit down with me now and rest please. You look very tired! I believe this will be an excellent spot to provide us some shade.

Oh, look, dear traveler! I see the crowd is already gathering along the hillside, this must be the right place alright."

As they looked down the dusty path, lined with sparse scrub and a few olive trees, they hear the noise of the crowd nearing. Their excitement increases as the crowd gathers nearby.

How else can we know what was really different in those days then for us to take advantage of this rare opportunity to witness Jesus with those who were seeking him?

"My friend, I believe I can see Jesus approaching the hill and what a trail of people are following him", said the weary companion as he spread his cloak on the ground. *Why the crowd seems to be pressing him on every side and, still, he teaches them, but where is his Bible?*

*Oh how silly of me! I forget that most of them are illiterate and simple
hard working folk. There was no Bible, as we know it in our day. Ah, good,
it seems everyone is finally settling on the hillside around him and Jesus is
starting to teach."*

Jesus sat on a large elevated pile of stones before the people.
Some children immediately began running towards him, but the
parents quickly grabbed them to prevent them from disturbing
the Master.

*"Look, dear companion, can you believe that Jesus is opening his arms
and motioning for the parents to allow the children to come to him. Do you
see that?"*

*"Do you realize, my friend, that in our modern church-age such things
would not be permitted. Wow! So much for our day's church nurseries and
Sunday schools as we know church to be."*

*"What? No! Jesus does not seem to mind at all and the children are
crawling up into his lap while he is teaching. Now, dear friend, that is
something our ministers would absolutely never tolerate!"*

"I am so glad you are my dear companion and with me on this
amazing journey. You always come so well prepared. Grab your
writing sack quickly and let's move a little closer so we can better
hear what Jesus is saying?"

As they resettled and the companion was busy rearranging his
writing materials, the crowd seemed to become disturbed that the
children were climbing all over Jesus. Then, as if the children
were not bothering him, Jesus began to address the crowd;

*"Listen my friend. Jesus seems to be speaking to the crowd again and if I
am not mistaken, it is something about the children. Please, stop shuffling
your notes! Be still, so we can hear what he is saying now!"*

Jesus looked intently at the crowd while holding a small child
in his arms while he began speaking;

*"Suffer the little children to come unto me for such is the kingdom of
God."*

*"Companion, did you hear that? Now, what on earth could Jesus mean
by that statement I wonder? I believe he has more to say."*

The crowd appeared to be spell-bound while the disciples began to distribute a few baskets of fish and bread to the multitude, as directed by Jesus.

"How on earth can a few baskets of bread and fish feed so many people? Such a small amount for such an enormous and hungry crowd? Wait! I believe Jesus is about to say something more."

Jesus speaks:

"I am able to do nothing of myself, independently of my own accord, but only as I am taught by God to do. I do not seek or consult my own will. I have no desire to do what is pleasing to myself, my own aim and purpose, is but to do only the will and pleasure of the One who sent me"

"Dear friend, did Jesus just answer our question? Surely, he does not mean what I think he means!"

"Do my ears deceive me, dear companion? Did you hear what I think I heard him say? Why, I believe he basically told everyone that he, Jesus Christ, cannot live the Christian life himself! I must be mistaken!"

"But surely Jesus can live the Christian life and, in fact, did so while on earth. I mean, if he cannot do so, then what hope do any of us have?"

The companion lowered his head in anguish. As the two travelers gathered their things and prepared to leave before the multitude dispersed, they could not resist looking back one more time while walking away.

They were both shocked at what they saw! They witnessed a miracle happening before their eyes! They were greatly overwhelmed and unable to speak or move briefly!

"Did you see that, my friend, did you see what the disciples were collecting from the crowd after they all ate until they were full? Why, there must be thousands here! Look at those overflowing baskets of bread and fish they are collecting after everyone has eaten."

They almost stumbled over each other trying to recover from what they had witnessed as they made their way down the hillside.

"How in the world do we return to our century, my friend, after what we have just witnessed? How can we sit quietly in a pew and pretend that God

is present after what we have just personally seen and be content with traditional Christianity?

Oh my dear companion! We are well pass the point of being content with our century's religion. And with that statement Jesus made that not even he, of his own, can live the Christian life. Well, we certainly have a great deal to think about and sort through when we get back.

Oh, here! Let me help you with that heavy burden on your back, You have carried that burden for quite some time now. After all, would I be a very good friend if I allowed you to struggle with your own burden and do not attempt to help you with it? Here, let me take that. I'll carry your burden the rest of the way."

"Thank you, my friend!"

-10-
CHILDHOOD - LAUNCHPAD INTO TOMORROW

Jesus said,

"Let the little children come to me, and do not hinder them, for the kingdom of heaven belongs to such as these!" (Matthew 19)

After many decades of global ministry, I remain amazed how easily we are deceived by the enemy!

All that the enemy has to do is to utilize well-intentioned Christians to misquote scripture and deny their own worldly biases and sinful nature.

In many situations, all that is needed is a person of a respected reputation, or position, like a pastor, teacher, close friend, or perhaps even a government leader, to quote a little scripture and set forth goals and agendas that tickle our ears. Soon thereafter, we also become one of their adherents.

When it comes to human suffering, pain, abuse and trauma; the buffet of choices is vast! America is at the top of the list when it comes to Bible-quoting Christians.

However, to find those who, after years of church attendance, possess a realistic biblical foundation, an understanding of the human soul, and a life that reflects Jesus and God, as presented in the whole of the Bible, is indeed very rare.

Meet The Other You

Let's take a few moments to review how our brain and mind attempt to manage pain and suffering.

After all, are we not provided with a biblical declaration regarding our Creator and his masterpiece of creation, the human composition?

"I will praise thee; for I am fearfully and wonderfully made: marvelous are thy works and that my soul knows well." (Psalms 139)

Few Christians understand, or even have an interest in, how our soul interacts with our human composition and the world. This lack of interest, unfortunately, is one of the primary causes of a self-centered, weak, and unstable relationship with our Lord and others.

Whenever our life does not work out quite like we think it should, we find ourselves asking, **Where were you God?** During such times of suffering and pain, the very same scriptures we loved to read and quote suddenly make no sense to us.

Past hurts and trauma do not automatically vanish, or cease to impact our lives, once we receive the rebirth, no more than our human biases and sensual appetites disappear. It is indeed a process of continual surrender, dying-to-self and an increasing intimacy with our Lord.

In the book; <u>Re-Discovering the Image of God for Your Life</u>, I discuss what is meant in the Bible when it proclaims Adam was created in the **image** and **likeness** of the triune Godhead.

Let us take a closer look at Adam for a moment;

*"And God said, Let **us** make man in **our** image, after **our** likeness…" (Genesis 1)*

Immediately, the reader is introduced not to a God in the singular tense, but to a triune (three-fold) being who operates in three distinct manifestations, all co-equal with one another, yet within separate aspects of one ministry.

Let's review the creation account to better understand Adam's three-fold human composition;

"And the Lord God formed man of the dust of the ground (flesh), and breathed into his nostrils the breath of life (spirit), and he became a living being (soul)." (Genesis 2)

After the Creator fashioned Adam from the elements of the earth, his physical composition, there was still no sign of life in him. Why?

Before I address this question, consider with me the fact that today's world culture, especially America, is preoccupied with the care and appearance of the physical body to an excess. The preoccupation with the body is a form of human worship and dates back centuries.

We spend a great deal of money and surgeries, not to mention a tremendous amount of time, to ensure that our appearance is pleasing to others.

We give our body the best medical care that is available, we attempt to live in accordance with environmentally-produced beliefs and experiences that tell us what will help us be more acceptable and successful. We immerse our sensual appetites with basically whatever our body craves.

Now, let's get back to our generational father, Adam. Notice Adam did not move after the body was completed. The body remained lifeless while on the ground from which it was formed.

This, dear reader, is our key intersect point, the point at which we may acquire a deeper understanding of who we really are and who we really are not!

In other words, whoever you may see, talk with, touch, smell, and have a relationship with is not the real person! It is, at this point, that we must begin to grasp the scientific and biblical truth regarding **our identity** that the scripture places before us;

"And the Lord God formed man of the dust of the ground, and breathed into his nostrils the breath of life, and man became a living soul." (Genesis 2)

Meet Your Carnal Soul Person

Once God breathed into Adam's nostrils the **breath of life**, then, the motionless mass of flesh began to move and became a living being, but not until this was accomplished.

What is the meaning of this phrase, the breath of life, that gave animation and life to the lifeless earth-man lying on the ground?

†A careful study of both the Old and New Testaments, regarding the use of the word breath, will reveal it often represents the spirit-person encased within our body.

In other words, Adam was not a living being until the spirit-person was placed in him; therefore, your human spirit is the real YOU.

It is much like a person putting on a spacesuit. The spacesuit is not the man, the man is inside. The spacesuit enables the person within it to move, breathe, live and communicate in an environment which is foreign to its natural habitat.

So, it is with our human spirit who is housed within the spacesuit of our human flesh with all its associated components.

Cults, like satanism, well understand this reality and use it to their advantage. Is it not absolutely amazing that Christians are so naïve and unknowledgeable when it comes to the spiritual aspects of the human composition?

†When our earthly days are over, it is substantiated by scripture that our spirit-person separates from our body; consequently, this disconnection causes the fleshly, outer shell, to die.

Once our spirit detaches from the body, the body can no longer function even though all the physical components may still be operational at the time of separation.

Our heavenly Father's heart must ache when He has made the supreme sacrifice that was necessary through the death of his son, Jesus at Calvary; yet, millions of people globally choose to continue to live destitute and miserable soul lives.

The Soul Bridge

†Now, if our spirit-person is to able to communicate and live through our physical body and effectively utilize its intricate

neurophysiological network to navigate through this earthly realm, there must be added to this equation a method of connecting it to the outside world through the physical body; this method is the human soul.

†This is precisely the point where our amazing and mysterious soul, with its intricate processes, enters into our equation.

The term soul has several meanings in scripture depending upon the context of where it is located. For the purpose of this present analogy, the soul is to be understood as the human composite of the intellect, the will and its power of choice, with its emotional internet of connections throughout the human composition.

I refer to the soul here as the **bridge** because it enables our spirit-person to communicate and interact with the world through the body within the limitations of our relationship with the spirit realm.

Another amazing function of the soul is its ability to provide two-way communication between the human and the spirit realm; however, there are directionality issues involved.

What are these directionality issues, you may wonder? It is at this very point we cannot begin to comprehend the complexity of our human composition as a dualistic being.

To begin to develop a deeper understanding of the significance of our two-fold composition, our intellectual pursuit is limited to our relationship with our Creator through the indwelling Holy Spirit.

The specifics of which I speak, are little understood and less known by the global population of traditional Christianity today.

Preset Spiritual Laws

† Just as the earth has its own natural laws which govern its operation, laws like gravity which, if defied, will exact a penalty for such defiance; the spirit realm, likewise, is under the

government of preset spiritual laws that will also exact spiritual consequences if violated.

A person who has not been born-again in accordance with John, chapter 3, is incapable of correctly connecting with the realm of God except through a plea for mercy and surrender.

Only through a reconnection with God through the rebirth process can this reconnection occur; however, the natural birth-person can easily connect with the realm of spiritual darkness.

Why? Because access to the kingdom of darkness is an open portal through which the human intersects with it whether through deception or an intentional action.

Regardless of what mask Satan hides behind, occult, religion, government, prosperity etc. it is designed to be an open access point for infiltration by the enemy. This intersect point, we are warned in scripture, is easily accessible to humanity through human curiosity and ignorance; whether the person is conscious of it or not.

✝The only way to control this infiltration by evil is to allow the Lord to control our lives and to submit to his divine will for our lives. This is not a one step process, nor is it an instant thing that occurs at the rebirth.

The Creator expects each of us to cooperate with his revealed will for our lives as clearly available in his Word though continual teaching and personalized application by the Holy Spirit.

This process develops a progressive and continual setting-apart of our own will through our continual willful surrender, dying-to-self, as we pursue learning to walk in the Spirit and not fall victim to our birth-person's sensual appetites.

A Brief Tour Through Your Soul

The time has arrived to take you through the control center of the human composition, the central hub wherein all life processes and external interactions are regulated and determined. This tour will take you into a highly restricted area where very few seldom visit. Ready?

Every belief you form is dependent upon this control center. Even your emotions and feelings are closely reviewed and regulated in this busy twenty-four hour processing center.

Its encoded neurological messages will be relayed throughout your entire being and they will ultimately determine your behavior, your environmental interactions and your destiny.

Your future decisions will be developed from an intricate review of **billions of memory bits per second** which contain past experiences with special attached chemical codes, commands, that decide how to manage life.

This integrated circuitry of chemical and electrical impulses will determine, with lightning speed, what behaviors are needed for every situation.

The soul is your twenty-four hour strategic command center. Humanly speaking, the results of this intricate process will determine the quality of your tomorrow.

Memory Storage Vaults

Your memory's storage vaults contain classified experiences of all significant past events, including hurts, pain, and trauma. Your future, psychologically speaking, will evolve from your childhood experiences, for better or worse.

How you interact with your environment, your family, your work associates, your friends and yes, those who have hurt you, will largely be determined from the assessments and coding of each event by your soul.

So, how can we forgive those we believe have hurt us when we continually experience defeat after defeat? Such an act of **holistic restoration** can only occur if it is generated first from your spirit-person who has experienced the rebirth in accordance with the Gospel of John, chapter three.

> *Train up a child in the way he **should** go, when he is old he will not depart from it."*
> *(Proverbs 22:6)*

So often, this verse is misconstrued to mean if you raise a child in the Christian faith, he will not depart from it in later years.

Unfortunately, the insertion of the word **should** does not accurately identify what the ancient language was stating. It is more of an admonition to raise our children in the faith; however, they still possess the power of choice to decide the course of their lives.

The aspect of this scripture, which I wish to focus on here, is actually the reverse of the traditional interpretation of this scripture.

After working with individuals and families over years, many children are increasingly living rebellious and self-destructive lifestyles after leaving home; some even experience premature death as a result of such lifestyles.

Even more complex are situations in which children perceive the environmental interactions of the caregivers quite differently than how the parents perceive them to be.

The emotional and mental devastation, not to mention the physical aspect, that occurs within a child who develops within an unstable environment, is incomprehensible.

Many of these children grow-up and enter life with the expectation they will magically produce the good life without the typical emotional, psychological, and spiritual childhood luggage of their past childhoods.

Instability and **insecurity** within their homes, whether it was intentional or not, will provide the fertile soil for the production of a **broken spirit** within a child. The **do as I say, not as I do** that often modeled by parents is hypocrisy and it rejects the heart of the whole counsel of God.

This author was raised in such a home environment and although my parents loved me; nevertheless, their own addictions and emotional instability greatly damaged all of the children in various ways.

Fear, insecurity, an apprehension of what might happen next, are the frequent results of growing-up in an eggshell environment and they often produce emotional instability, and feelings of being unloved and unwanted.

These become the prime ingredients for a self-sabotaging and unstable adult life. Eventually, these will rupture into the adult's life and begin to sabotage their probability for happiness and purpose.

Children who emerge from abusive and insecure childhoods are launched into the world without a clue how to live a productive life, much less have intimacy with God whom they have never seen modeled by their parents.

Often, these children most likely will unconsciously reproduce a similar unstable family environment in their attempt to have a family. Some may **overcompensate** for their own lack of a secure home environment, which can prove to be equally as damaging.

Nothing is more astonishing than our mind, which includes the brain. It is the **reception and distribution center** for the daily processing of approximately **400 billion bits of information per second**.

Therefore, we need to take the time to obtain a clearer and deeper understanding of what really happens to us when trauma strikes in our lives.

Remember, much of what sabotages our lives is not available to our conscious awareness; therefore, this is when trained Christian assistance is frequently required.

Perception Activates the Alarms

The manner in which we interpret life's events is indeed a very complex process. It is based upon a cycle of things that continuous interplay with one another. All of these are in the area of our human neurological internet.

Two people can experience the same event; however, they will most likely react in completely different ways. **Perception**, simply stated, is the process of interpreting everything that happens to us in life.

This process is active within an infant; however, the interactive mechanisms are more chemical in nature with little interpretation of the events. These are stored and will later be developed.

Our perception develops over years and will become the building blocks of our belief system and how we interpret the events of life.

Eventually, over many years, our memory will store a massive amount of life-experiences along with residual correlated reactions.

This **memory library** will contain each negative and positive experience, especially if it was a frequent occurrence. It will also attach associated smells, visuals, sounds, tastes and touch that occurred at that time.

Here is a practical example of this complex subconscious process;

Mary, a fictitious name, came to see me regarding her explosive emotional outbursts that were creating discord in her home and workplace.

When I asked her to describe what set-off these outbursts, she replied she had no idea. After further dialogue, I discovered she is the youngest child of a family of four siblings.

She continued to explain by the time she was born, her mother had become very fragile and would explode with angry outbursts. These frequent and unpredictable outbursts usually were followed by some type of dominating and controlling behavior.

She further explained that her father was away a great deal on business trips and many of them were overnight or longer.

After discussing her current family and work situation, it became apparent, whenever certain people would interact with he in a similar fashion as her mother, that Mary would respond in anger and even an uncontrollable outburst, sometimes followed by harsh and hurtful words.

A Peek Behind The Scenes

I believe it is time to go back stage behind Mary's daily events, in a manner of speaking, to better understand how her soul became a crucial participant in such detrimental explosions.

Who Is In Charge?

†The **front lobe** of our brain, the prefrontal cortex, is the entry point for most environmental input. Whatever happens externally must process through the doors of the frontal part of our brain.

Herein is the area where our conscious awareness resides. All processing of incoming sensory information occurs here along with the interpretation and meaning of language.

†Whenever trauma occurs, the hormone **adrenaline** pulses throughout the body to prepare the muscular system for a **flight, or fight response**.

†The **Limbic system** of the brain is like your ever-ready emergency team, your rescue squad. It is activated during an emergency by regulating the emotional and motivational aspects of the body's alert response system.

†This process is of vital importance because it will implant a complete detailed memory of the event, which most likely will release aspects of it overtime back into our conscious awareness.

As a self-protective procedure, it will attempt to seal-off the pain of a traumatic event within an **amnesic barrier**; however, it is not designed for long-term storage and eventually will breakdown and leak portions of the memory back into the stream of our conscious awareness.

Your Soul Keeps Score

The purpose of this brief overview of the processing aspects of soul hopefully help provide a clearer understanding of its amazing complexity.

Once a threat occurs, the self-defense response of our soul attempts to minimize the impact of it. This entire automatic process is very complex and detailed.

In later years, it may eventually rupture through our conscious awareness and intrude into our present life with all its associated sensory anchors including any original emotions and pain from the original trauma.

Have You Met Your Inner Child?

Twenty-first century cultural and social pressures insist that we grow-up and abandon anything remotely childish.

However, it only takes a casual panoramic view of our world today to discover much of our so-called adult behavior is, in fact childish behavior.

Self-sabotaging and destructive behavior wear many masks in today's society. Generally speaking, much of our adult behavior, if closely scrutinized, will reveal residual childish impulsivity and ego-centric emotions and behaviors.

Often, throughout life, we exhibit neediness, self-indulgence, dependency, and a range of fears and emotional insecurities. Many of these may be fueled by deep feelings of abandonment and rejection.

The Bible, our textbook reliable authority on the human composition, is permeated with solid teaching regarding the expanding buffet of infantile and childish emotional insensitivity and instabilities within the adult.

If truth were accepted and realized, we all very much still house within our souls the emotions and behaviors of our childhood tears. I have found the behavior and emotions of that inner child is usually around the age of five years old.

The majority of adults are so preoccupied with their goals and sensual appetites, they race through life unaware that much of their behavior, emotions and even costly impulsive decisions emerge from the mindset of our inner child.

Why? Because there are still dark areas of our being that are unhealed from past suffering and hurts. In other words, most of us still need deep healing and an the experience of God's genuine acceptance, love and approval. The rebirth does not automatically wipe the slate clean of all past hurts; it is a cooperative effort.

The Illusion of Adulthood

In reality, the majority of adults in our country and throughout the world are not adults at all, except chronologically.

†The quality of our childhood will often determine the quality of our inner child and the degree of its infiltrating childish exhibitions and needs through us as adults.

†The inner child is simply that unhealed part of our soul that still feels unsafe, insecure, unwanted and in search of real intimacy, acceptance and unconditional love.

Well, I see our journey has reached an end. Together, we have briefly explored the importance and centrality of the power of childhood in our lives and we have hopefully somewhat realized the deep inner need and urgency for us to reconnect with our Creator and Lord for holistic healing.

Our childhood was indeed our launching pad into adulthood. It begins at the point of conception. The start of the inner construction of this launching site actually began generationally with our parental bloodlines.

The pervasive error that Satan has systematically seeded into the church over the centuries is that once a person becomes a Christian all things become new, old things pass away. This too is a distortion of the true meaning of this scripture.

It is erroneously misinterpreted to mean the past cannot impact our present or future once we become a child of God through Jesus Christ.

Like so many other erroneous twists of divine scripture, these systematic distortions have eroded divine truth and provided a slippery slope on which untold numbers of God's people have fallen victim, some towards their ultimate destruction.

This book, in part, represents my own journey of recovery, as well as those of an innumerable number of others with whom I have been privileged to meet and work with over decades.

Like myself, they emerged from unstable childhoods in with varying degrees of **soul shattering**. These activate self-sabotaging emotions, thoughts, and behaviors throughout the course of our lives.

My own life's direction has been primarily driven in a self-sabotaging manner by my own unstable childhood. I have purposely focused on portions of my life in hopes it may prayerfully assist you to move forward towards holistic healing for your own shattering which is only available in Jesus Christ.

What I was unaware of, for the greater part of my adult life, was that I attempted to discover healing for my own brokenness; my own inner child who deeply suffered so much pain and heartache by immersing myself in attempting to help others heal what I could not do for myself.

The Power of Childhood is, of course, a portion of my own story and I realize this; however, I expect it may as well represent a part of your story as well.

What I have written on these pages are true and factual; however there is so much more that could be said about this lifetime journey we are all traveling.

Whenever we make a commitment to heal, there is always a price to pay; however, when we decide not to do anything about our own brokenness, there is an even greater price to pay. Typically, our loved ones and those we care about may, likewise, will be forced to share our pain with us.

The major difference between the two, I suppose, could be the price those you care about and love will also pay when we allow denial to win and we choose to do nothing about our intrusive past hurts, hurts that eventually will rupture into the lives of others as well our self.

Let me gently urge you, dear one, if you are one of those who can identify with any part of what I have tried to share, to be encouraged. There is healing available!

If looking back at your life represents disappointment and defeat, then let me encourage you to place another foot forward and determine to pursue your healing, if not for you, then for those you care about and love.

I have desired that you know my heart in this urgent matter and I assure you it is my sincere prayer our journey together has proven to be an encouragement to you and, hopefully, it has given you a deeper insight into the awesome power of our childhood, for better or for worse.

May this book be the beginning of your divine intersect with God!

ABOUT THE AUTHOR

Dr. Stanfield writes with decades of experience as a researcher, crisis counselor, pastor, biblical psychologist and educator.

As a past founder of an international trauma center, he weaves years of teaching, training, ministry, and personal healing into each of his books with a passion to help others.

Today, he spends much of his time writing, teaching, and he continues to be active in private ministry.

Dr. Stanfield and his wife Nancy reside in Florida.

Should you desire to contact me, my email address is (**dr.lwstanfield@gmail.com**)

www.ingramcontent.com/pod-product-compliance
Lightning Source LLC
Chambersburg PA
CBHW051359280526
45784CB00007B/3016